A CHAMPION GAME PLAN FOR LIFE

PRESTON BROWN

authorHOUSE®

AuthorHouse™
1663 Liberty Drive
Bloomington, IN 47403
www.authorhouse.com
Phone: 1 (800) 839-8640

Published by AuthorHouse 03/12/2018

ISBN: 978-1-5462-3091-5 (sc)
ISBN: 978-1-5462-3090-8 (hc)
ISBN: 978-1-5462-3089-2 (e)

Library of Congress Control Number: 2018902337

Print information available on the last page.

CONTENTS

Acknowledgments ix

Introduction xi

Game Plan For Today: Staying Connected.. 1

Game Plan for Today: Take another Step.. 3

Game Plan for Today: Overcoming the What-Ifs... 5

Game Plan for Today: The Man in the Mirror 7

Game Plan for Today: Faith in the Right Place... 8

Game Plan for Today: Needless Worries... 9

Game Plan for Today: From Hate to Hope 10

Game Plan for Today: If God Be for Us... 12

Game Plan for Today: The Power of Forgiveness 14

Game Plan for Today: Preparing for Salvation.. 15

Game Plan For Today: Getting what We Deserve 17

Game Plan for Today: A Guided Life... 18

Game Plan for Today: A New Level of Praise 19

Game Plan for Today: Gifts and Talents 21

Game Plan for Today: Everyday Faith.. 23

Game Plan for Today: Wisdom.. 25

Game Plan for Today: Know Your Why Before Your What 27

Game Plan for Today: It's written all over your face 29

Game Plan for Today: No Fear 31

Game Plan for Today: Before You Build the Fire.. 33

Game Plan for Today: A Marriage That Works... 35

Game Plan for Today: Anxious for Nothing 37

Game Plan for Today: Getting what you want 38

Game Plan for Today: What's Holding You Back 40

Game Plan for Today: Be Encouraged 42

Game Plan for Today: Being Accountable 44

Game Plan for Today: According to His Purpose 46

Game Plan for Today: Strong Finish 48

Game Plan for Today: The Purpose for Obedience 50

Game Plan for Today: Be Patient..52

Game Plan for Today: From Blaming to Claiming 54

Game Plan for Today: No Regrets 56

Game Plan for Today: The Abundant Life 58

Game Plan for Today: The Narrow Path 60

Game Plan for Today: Better 62

Game Plan for Today: Don't Wait for Tomorrow 64

Game Plan for Today: Deep Roots 66

Game Plan For Today: The Faith Bridge 68

Game Plan for Today: Turn the Lights on 70

Game Plan For Today: A Relationship that Matters 71

Game Plan For Today: The Certainty of Hope 73

Game Plan for Today: Winning the Spiritual Battles 75

Game Plan for Today: Change Is Good 77

Game Plan for Today: Be Thankful 78

Game Plan for Today: Payday..80

Game Plan for Today: The Setup 81

Game Plan for Today: Make Time 83

Game Plan for Today: Good Fruit 85

Game Plan for Today: Getting Your Priorities in Order 86

Game Plan for Today: Forgiving Yourself................................88

Game Plan for Today: Are We There Yet? 90

Game Plan for Today: Good Intensions................................92

Game Plan for Today: The Choice Is Yours 94

Game Plan for Today: God's Presence in Your Life...............96

Game Plan for Today: Strength from Weakness 98

Game Plan for Today: Seizing the Opportunities 100

Game Plan for Today: Realizing Your Full Potential 102

Game Plan for Today: I Will Not Be Moved 104

Game Plan for Today: Great Faith......................................106

Game Plan for Today: Holding on to Your Faith 107

Game Plan for Today: A Life Alignment.............................109

Game Plan for Today: Buckle Up 110

Game Plan for Today: A Heart That Pleases God................112

Game Plan for Today: Getting the Weeds Out 114

Game Plan for Today: Looking More like God....................116

Game Plan for Today: Cost and Rewards 118

Game Plan For Today: Providing Comfort For Others.........120

ACKNOWLEDGMENTS

First of all, I would like to thank God, from whom all blessings flow, because without Him I can do nothing.

For my wife, Terry, who has been a great supporter, as most wives should be. Thank you for always being there. I love you very much.

Thank you to my mother-in-law, Laura Williams, who encouraged me to go back to work after her daughter, who was my wife of thirty years, passed away. Because of that, I was able to continue to do what God has called me to do, which is to bring Him glory.

I want to thank Pastor Tomasi Muhomba, for giving me the opportunity to preach at the morning service. It was thanks to this great man of God that I could begin writing about the goodness that God can bring to your life.

Also, a very special thanks to Dorothy Houston, the editor-in-chief of *The Valley Weekly*, which allowed me to develop *"Champion Game Plan for Life.*

I also want to thank my sister Lori Mirabal, who encouraged me not to wait any longer and "just do it." Thank you, Lori.

Finally, I want to thank the greatest support group (next to my wife) that anyone could have, Pastor Sam Wilson and his wife (my daughter) Kristen, Pastor Wayne Dickens and his wife (my daughter) Stacey, and all my grandchildren, Kayna, Sam Jr., Naomi, Cannon, and Duke.

INTRODUCTION

So many of our youth today are on the "cusp" of greatness and of failure. It's as if they are one circumstance away from having the abundant life that God wants us to have. Whether it's because of an unexpected pregnancy, the death of a parent, or maybe just getting caught up with the wrong crowd, greatness eludes them. That's why I believe that in today's world, we all need a plan to help us navigate through the good times as well as the bad times—a plan that can be a "bridge" over troubled waters when they appear.

When I played football, whether it was in high school, college, or a professional league, we would have a "game plan." Having a game plan gave our team the best chance to win the game. With this game plan, we would learn the strengths and the weaknesses of the enemy (excuse me), the team that we were facing. When you have a plan, you will be able to handle whatever situation that you find yourself in.

Romans 8:28 says, "And we know that in all things God works for the good of those who love Him, who have been called for his purpose." It goes on to say, "We are more than conquerors through Him who loves us" (Romans 8:37). But if we don't know this, the enemy can easily defeat us. John 10:10 says that the thief comes only to kill steal and destroy, but Jesus said, "I came that you might have an abundant life." I believe that having a *Champion Game Plan for Life* will take you to another level of excellence. We have to remember that "storms" are not always in the forecast. There will be test and trials that we will go through; however, having daily reminders to help us deal with certain issues in life can be extremely helpful. For example, the Bible tells us in James 1:2–4, "Consider it pure joy, my brothers and sisters whenever you face trials of many kinds because you know that the testing of your faith produces perseverance." Perseverance must finish its work so that you may be mature and complete, not lacking anything." (James 1:4) I never really understood that scripture until God revealed to me a "plan" for my life.

Remember that just as the cars and trucks that we drive require constant refuelling, we all need spiritual fuel as well. And that fuel comes from hearing and reading the word of God every day. These small chapters offer strategies or plans for your life, so I pray that you read them and that you would be affected by them in such a way that you will have the faith to do something about it. James 1:22–23 says, "Do not merely listen to the word, and so deceive yourselves. Do what it says. Anyone who listens to the word but does not do what it says is like a man who looks at his face in the mirror and, after looking at himself, goes away and immediately forgets what he looks like." I truly believe that having a *Champion Game Plan for Life* will help our youth, as well as our adults, know God's word so that we can be obedient to His word and bring Him glory. Stay encouraged, my brothers and sisters.

GAME PLAN FOR TODAY: STAYING CONNECTED

John 15:5 says, "I am the vine; you are the branches. If you remain in me and I in you. You will bear much fruit; apart from me you can do nothing."

Today we live in a society of extreme technology. People are constantly talking on their cell phones, texting, playing games, and never looking up to acknowledge other people. Not only are we addicted to our cell phones, but it seems that we have to be entertained at all times. We live in a society where people are afraid of being bored. But we have to realize and understand that this is another trick by the enemy to distract us from being in fellowship with God and with other people. You see, the more we isolate ourselves from people, the less accountable we are for our actions. On the other hand, the more we connect with God, the more we will want to connect with other people. You see God desires us to be in fellowship with Him. He also wants us to have balance in our lives. So don't allow the longing to be entertained keep you from wanting to be in the presence of God. Let's start giving Him the time that He deserves, and remember to stay connected to the only power source that we need, which is Jesus. Stay encouraged, my brothers and sisters.

Prayer: Dear God, help us to be aware of the distractions that keep us from being connected with you.

GAME PLAN FOR TODAY: TAKE ANOTHER STEP

Jeremiah 29:11 says, "For I know the plans I have for you, plans to prosper you and not to harm you, plans to give you hope and a future."

What if every time you prayed, God answered your prayers immediately? I don't know about you, but I would be praying all the time. But God wants to know this: Will you still pray if He doesn't answer your prayers when you want Him to? Will you still trust Him? Will you still believe in Him?

You see, sometimes our progress is not as obvious as we would like it to be. But just because your promise isn't obvious, this does not mean your faith isn't working. We all need to learn to take another step, even if nothing appears to be happening. When God allows us to be in a certain situation and we think that it's taking too long for Him to answer our prayers, maybe God wants us to be less focused on the outcome and more focused on our obedience. The outcome is God's responsibility. Obedience is ours. So take another step, and you may just walk on past your problems. Stay encouraged, my brothers and sisters.

Prayer: Heavenly Father, give us the courage that we need to take another step of faith when you call us to do so.

GAME PLAN FOR TODAY: OVERCOMING THE WHAT-IFS

Exodus 4:1, Moses says, "What if they don't believe me or listen to me?"

For many of us, it's not so much about what we have its more about how we use what we have. So many people have so much potential and do not know what they are capable of until God reveals it to them. And the way He reveals it to us is through our prayers and our circumstances. If we walk in faith, everything that we need is within our reach. In Exodus 4:2, God asked Moses what was in his hand. Moses replied that it was a staff. So God is saying to Moses that he already has what he needs in his hand. All he needs to do is learn how to use it. When you begin to think that you don't have what you need, you will begin to believe it. That's why we need to learn to speak life to our circumstances and our situations and start believing in the promises of God, which is "I can do all things through Christ, who gives me strength" (Philippians 4:13). So when people don't believe in you, believe in yourself. God was telling Moses, and all of us, to not let the what-ifs keep us from our destinies. Don't let the what-ifs keep you from being all that God has called you to be and don't let the what-ifs keep you from your blessings from God. Stay encouraged, my brothers and sisters.

Prayer: Dear God, give us the strength that we need to overcome the doubts and fears that we have.

GAME PLAN FOR TODAY: THE MAN IN THE MIRROR

Matthew 7:3, Jesus says, "Why do you look at the speck of sawdust in your brother's eye and pay no attention to the plank that is in your own eye?"

When it comes to dealing with people and their issues, we tend to look through a magnifying glass at their problems and their mistakes. But what we should be using is a mirror so we can see our own mistakes. You see, we all have issues, and sometimes when we see something in a person that makes us angry or upset, we are really looking at something inside ourselves that we have to deal with. So we have to decide, "Am I going to focus on their issues or my issues?" The key to loving our neighbors as we love ourselves is to put down the magnifying glass, pick up the mirror, and ask God, "What do I need to change in my life to be all that I can be for your glory?" Remember: if we want to make this world a better place, we have to begin with the man in the mirror. Stay encouraged, my brothers and sisters.

Prayer: Heavenly Father, allow us to not judge one another but instead love one another.

GAME PLAN FOR TODAY: FAITH IN THE RIGHT PLACE

Second Timothy 1:7 says, "For God has not given us a spirit of fear and timidity but of power, love, and self-discipline."

We've all come this far by faith, leaning on the Lord. But sometimes our faith is tied to the way that we want things to happen, not the way that God wants them to happen. For example, some people never finish school because their circumstances change. This might be due to an unexpected pregnancy, the death of a loved one, or financial problems. So many things can get us off track and lead us off the path that God wants us to walk. But if we put our trust in God's plan and don't give up on His promises, we will make it. And the way that we make it is to put our faith in the right place, which is in God's capable hands. We have to say to ourselves, "I believe that God is working in my life right now." So, no matter what circumstances you may find yourselves in, don't let your faith depend on the way that you want things to happen. Stay encouraged, my brothers and sisters.

Prayer: Most gracious and loving Father, continue to lead us and guide us in the way you would like us to go.

GAME PLAN FOR TODAY: NEEDLESS WORRIES

Philippians 4:6 says, "Do not be anxious about anything, but in every situation, by prayer and petition, with thanksgiving, present your request to God."

One of the reasons we feel anxious about things is that we are not thankful for what we already have. In this verse, Paul is saying that if you never stop and pray and thank God for what you already have, you will always be anxious. So many Christians today are anxious about so many things in this world. It may be our jobs, our marriages, or our children. But instead of being anxious, Paul is saying that we should pray about everything. You see, we have to know what it means for God to be for us and train our hearts and minds to be anxious for nothing. Remember: if we are following God's purpose for our lives, there is no reason for us to have these needles worries. Stay encouraged, my brothers and sisters.

Prayer: Loving Father, take away our needless worries and help us replace them with the need to be thankful for the many blessings that we already have.

GAME PLAN FOR TODAY: FROM HATE TO HOPE

Romans 12:9 says, "Love must be sincere, hate what is evil, cling to what is good."

It has been said that before we can make any real changes in our lives, we have to be motivated by hate. Yes, hate, because hate is a powerful emotion. It means to dislike something intensely. But here is the thing: we should hate what is evil. We should hate the things that we do to ourselves that harm us. Like smoking, or eating too much, or watching pornography. All these things need to be motivated by a healthy dose of hate. We have to learn to hate the bad things that are going on in our lives. You see, there is a healthy way to hate. We should hate racism. We should hate when people take advantage of other people. Psalm 119:113 says, "I hate the double-minded but I love your law." Until we hate something enough, we will never make the change to do something about it. Therefore, whenever you are struggling with something you want to change, you have to hate it. Hate it because it is keeping you from bringing God the glory that He deserves and that you deserve. Stay encouraged, my brothers and sisters.

Prayer: Loving Father, take away the things in our lives that are causing us to harm ourselves as well as others around us. In Jesus's name, we pray.

GAME PLAN FOR TODAY:
IF GOD BE FOR US

Genesis 29:31 says, "When the Lord saw that Leah was not loved (by Jacob), He enabled her to conceive, but Rachel remained childless."

The two foundations that drive most of our lives are approval and achievement. But we all need to remember that in God's eyes we are more than the "likes" that we get on Facebook. We are more than the "views" that we get on YouTube. We are also more than the friends that we try to accumulate from various sources. You see, God is not concerned with our social status. God is concerned with what's going on the inside of us. God is concerned with matters of the heart. Whenever we start comparing our lives to those of other people, we end up frustrated, incomplete, and miserable. So for every person that has been in a relationship and knows the pain of being unwanted, God has a plan for you, because God selects what man rejects. Remember—God being here for us means more than the approvals and achievements of this world. You see, God has a word for the people that, for whatever reason, have not been chosen in this world. God says to all of us, "I will never leave you nor forsake you" (Hebrews 13:5). Therefore, when this world finds no interest in you, remember that God finds interest in you and He is interested in everything that you do. That's the kind of God that we serve. Stay encouraged, my brothers and sisters.

Prayer: Most gracious and loving Father, thank You for loving us just the way we are and refusing to leave us that way.

GAME PLAN FOR TODAY: THE POWER OF FORGIVENESS

Job 42:10 says, "After Job had prayed for his friends, the Lord restored his fortunes and gave him twice as much as he had before."

The Bible tells us to pray for our enemies and care enough about them to want to see them go to heaven. But it's interesting to me that so many Christians today are angry and upset over people who have hurt them. But we need to remember that "hurting people" hurt other people. They hurt others due to the pain they have in their own lives. So it's time to forgive those who have hurt you.

There is a song that goes, "I want a heart that forgives, a heart full of love, one with compassion like yours above, one that overcomes evil with goodness and love, like it never happens, never holding a grudge." I think this says it all. You see, the promises of God come with conditions. We can't be blessed and also be mad at everybody at the same time. Remember that love gives and forgives. Stay encouraged, my brothers and sisters.

Prayer: Dear God, help us to forgive those who have hurt us, even when we don't feel like it.

GAME PLAN FOR TODAY: PREPARING FOR SALVATION

Hebrews 9:27 says, "It is appointed that we will all die and face certain judgment."

Many people live as though there is no tomorrow, but tomorrow always comes. You see, death is something that none of us can avoid, but we want to make sure that when we do die, we end up in the right place. There is a popular song called "Live like You Were Dying." It talks about doing a number of amazing things, but none of them have anything to do with the afterlife. You see, death is something that we don't have to be afraid of, if we believe in God's word. The bottom line is: This is not our home, and we are not expected to be here forever. So we need to spend our time here on this earth preparing ourselves for our time that we will spend in heaven. Remember—salvation is for those who believe that Jesus came, died, and rose again for the sins of the whole world. And this salvation is not of ourselves but is a gift from God. We can't earn it, and we can't deserve it. We can only obtain it through accepting Jesus Christ as our Lord and Savior. Stay encouraged, my brothers and sisters.

Prayer: Most gracious and loving Father, help us to live like we were dying but with salvation in mind and to realize that this is not our home.

GAME PLAN FOR TODAY: GETTING WHAT WE DESERVE

Philippians 3:3 says we should put no confidence in the flesh.

No matter what accomplishments that we obtain, they are all from God. All the good that we do comes from God, not us. And when we do good things, God doesn't owe us anything. For example, if we get up every morning and pray for two hours, or if we read four chapters of the Bible every day, God doesn't owe us anything. These are things that we should be doing anyway. We need to get rid of this attitude in which we do something just to get something from God. It just doesn't work like that. You see, when we begin to understand that we don't deserve anything from God, then we will become happy and excited about everything that God does for us. Stay encouraged, my brothers and sisters.

Prayer: Dear God, help us to understand that our confidence is not in the things that we do but in the God that we serve.

GAME PLAN FOR TODAY: A GUIDED LIFE

Proverbs 3:8 says, "Acknowledge God in all your ways, and He will guide your steps."

I think that our lives would be more enjoyable if we knew how much God wanted to get involved. We don't need to settle for mediocrity when God has called us to excellence. The word mediocre implies a halfway point between success and failure. You see, when we delight ourselves in the Lord, He will give us the desires of our hearts, not the desires of our flesh. So much of life is about the choices we make, and there are principles that we need to live by to make those choices. One of the things we can start doing is to stop being miserable about things we can't do anything about. Let us all get the spirit of "dread" out of our lives. Sometimes we dread getting up in the morning, or we dread going to work, or we dread working out. Remember—dread is the opposite of hope. So we need to stay on the path that God is leading us on which leads to a beautiful life. Stay encouraged, my brothers and sisters.

Prayer: Loving Father, guide our steps while we run the race that you have set before us, in Jesus's name we pray.

GAME PLAN FOR TODAY: A NEW LEVEL OF PRAISE

First Peter 1:3–4 says, "Praise be to the God and Father of our Lord Jesus Christ! In His great mercy, He has given us new birth into a living hope through the resurrection of Jesus Christ from the dead and into an inheritance that can never perish spoil or fade."

As we read this text, we should all realize that Peter is showing us a new level of praise. Remember that Peter was the one who denied Jesus three times before the rooster crowed. And since Jesus died on the cross, there was no way for him to tell Jesus just how sorry he was for doing that. I can't imagine the pain and the hurt that he must have gone through. But the good news for Peter and for all of us is that Jesus did not perish on the cross. He lives—Christ Jesus lives today—and because he lives, we can face tomorrow. You see, Jesus forgave Peter, and now he has a new level of praise. There is a different kind of praise that you give when you are on the other side of the pain. Remember that your faith cannot be proven if you never go through any storms in your life. But don't focus on the distractions, focus on the journey. Stay encouraged, my brothers and sisters.

Prayer: Holy God, thank You for not only forgiving us but allowing us to be reconnected with you.

GAME PLAN FOR TODAY:
GIFTS AND TALENTS

Matthew 25:15 says, "To one he gave five talents of money, to another two talents, and to another one talent, each according to his ability."

D o you appreciate the gifts that God has given you, or do you always see the wrong things in your life? God wants us to be thankful for the gifts and talents that he has given us. That's why we can't afford to sit around and compare what we have to what others have. This behavior will only make us miserable. So it's important that we like ourselves as well as the gifts that God has blessed us with. When we do this, we can begin to like and appreciate other people as well.

Matthew 25:29 goes on to say, "For everyone who has will be given more, and he will have an abundance. Whoever does not have, even what he has will be taken from him."

When we look at this scripture, we see that God simply wants us to be thankful for what we have. Because when we do, more will be given. So let us also learn to enjoy the people who are in our lives—our friends, our families, our coworkers, people with whom we interact daily. Because friends and family members are gifts from God as well. But the only way that we can do this is to stop focusing on everything that is wrong with them. It's time to make a change and be part of the solution instead of part of the problem. Stay encouraged, my brothers and sisters.

Prayer: Loving Father, help us to appreciate the gifts and talents that you have blessed us with and help us to stop comparing what we have to what others have.

GAME PLAN FOR TODAY: EVERYDAY FAITH

Hebrews 11:1 says, "Now faith is confidence in what we hope for and assurance about what we do not see."

Sometimes we think that we need some kind of special knowledge to grow in our faith. However, what we need is the kind of faith that grows in our everyday life. We need the kind of faith that is adaptable to whatever circumstance or situations we are going through. I want a faith that you can use every day, not just on Sunday. I want a faith that deals with the everyday ups and downs of life. We also need a durable faith. We need a faith that is not held hostage by the outcome. Because as we read this scripture, faith is having confidence in what we do not see. If you could see it, then it wouldn't be faith. Remember, if you need a certain outcome to validate your faith, it's only a matter of time before you give up on your faith. That's why you need a faith that works even when your situation is not cooperating. We need a faith that works even though you don't know what is going to happen next. In other words, a faith that's not based on an outcome but based on an outlook. Stay encouraged, my brothers and sisters.

Prayer: Most gracious God, give us a faith that will endure through any kind of situation.

GAME PLAN FOR TODAY: WISDOM

James 3:13 says, "Who is wise and understanding among you? Let them show it by their good life, by deeds done in the humility that comes from wisdom."

Wisdom means doing now what you'll be happy with later in life. Wisdom means thinking things through. If you read Proverbs, you will see that wisdom involves "prudence," which means good management. It also involves discernment, which means looking beyond the "surface" of the matter and looking for a deeper meaning. You see, a proud person who thinks more of himself than he should does not have one drop of wisdom in him. Remember the rich young ruler who thought he knew it all, but when he asked Jesus the question about eternal life, it was revealed that not only did he not know the truth about himself' but he lacked the main thing he needed to get to heaven, which was he loved his wealth more than serving God. We will never have wisdom unless we desire and pursue wisdom on purpose. Wisdom comes from God, and He gives it freely if we ask for it. I have found that in my life, wisdom and peace are the most important things I can have. Because with the blessings of wisdom in your life it will bring forth the anointing that God wants us to have. Stay encouraged, my brothers and sisters.

Prayer: Dear God, grant us the wisdom that we need to bring you glory.

GAME PLAN FOR TODAY: KNOW YOUR WHY BEFORE YOUR WHAT

In Philippians 3:14, Paul says, "I press on toward the goal to win the prize for which God has called me heavenward in Christ Jesus."

We all need a sense of progress to continue achieving our goals in life—whether it be our jobs, our education, our exercise at the gym, or even our ministry. It can be hard to show up again and again when something is not working. We all need to see some kind of progress. Therefore, if progress is essential to our mental and spiritual growth, how do we make progress? Most of us would say that effort produces progress. For example, how do you expect to pass a test that you never study for? We need to apply effort to produce progress. But remember—effort alone will not produce progress. We also need direction. We need to know if we are headed in the right direction. Whenever you find yourself feeling frustrated, stressed, and burned out, perhaps you have been pointing your efforts in the wrong direction. I have found that the best way to point your efforts in the right direction is to discover your "why." When you begin to realize why you are doing what you are doing, you will remain headed in the right direction. Stay encouraged, my brothers and sisters.

Prayer: Gracious Father, give us the faith to continue on our spiritual journey, even when it looks as though we are not making any progress.

GAME PLAN FOR TODAY: IT'S WRITTEN ALL OVER YOUR FACE

In Numbers 6:24, we find the passage that says, "The Lord bless you and keep you, the Lord makes His face to shine upon you."

Our faces should reflect the God that we serve. So we can't have Him shine upon us and not change the way that we look. Our facial expression says a lot about the condition of our heart. So if you're happy and you know it, your face tells the story. So many people go through life with a cheerless countenance. They may not mean anything by it; perhaps they just look that way for whatever reason. Now I realize that in life, not every circumstance is going to make us happy, but if we are sons and daughters of the living God, our facial expressions should resemble that of our heavenly Father.

The way you look at life is written all over your face. I believe that if you stay in the presence of God, which means praying daily and staying in his word, He will turn your frown upside down. So if you are saved, look like it. If you are blessed, look like it. If you are redeemed, look like it. Remember that you don't have to say a word, because it's written all over your face. Stay encouraged, my brothers and sisters.

Prayer: Dear God, help us to let our lights shine so that others can see the good works that you have done for us.

GAME PLAN FOR TODAY:
NO FEAR

John 14:1 says, "Let not your hearts be troubled, believe in God, also believe in me."

Anytime we are in a "crisis" situation, we have to learn to control our emotions. This verse tells us that we can control our emotions. God would not give us a command that we could not follow. Therefore, if you really believe in the power of God, you will not panic. When we experience times of trouble, we have to use our faith. Now our faith can overcome all the fears that this world has to offer. But how do you know when you are in faith? I believe that you're in faith when you are facing a crisis and still have peace. Remember—the enemy doesn't want our stuff; he wants our peace. You see, when we panic, we release the power of fear, and fear is not from God. But when we have faith, we release the power of God into our lives. God will give us what we need to deal with any crisis in our lives. Now it's important to realize that the way you respond to a crisis will determine the outcome of your crisis. Remember when Jesus calmed the storm by saying "peace be still" (Mark 4:39) and all was calm. He can do the same in our lives if we put our trust and our faith in the one who controls the winds and the rains. Any time that we partner with Jesus we can rest assure that the outcome will be positive. So there is no need to fear when Jesus is near. Stay encouraged, my brothers and sisters.

Prayer: Heavenly Father, give us the peace that we need so that we can handle the challenges of life without being afraid

GAME PLAN FOR TODAY:
BEFORE YOU BUILD THE FIRE

First Corinthians 7:1–2 says, "It is good for a man not to marry. But since there is so much immorality, each man should have his own wife, and each woman her own husband."

You know, it is one thing to have passion, but it's another thing to act on it the right way. When we release passions intended for marriage that are outside the marriage, it's like building a fire with nothing to contain it. If you build a fire in the wrong place or if you put our passion in the wrong place, you will burn your home to the ground. In other words, everything that you and your spouse have built will go up in flames. I wonder how many people today could have avoided so many problems in their relationships, if someone had told them, "Before you build this fire in this other relationship, you need somewhere to contain this type of passion." But you will never find what you are looking for because it was never meant to be that way. Therefore, before you start that adulterous relationship, you need to realize where it's going. Before you start that "solo" relationship (i.e., watching pornography), you have to realize that you are playing with a fire that you can't contain. You see, God gives us all passion, and passion is good when channeled in the right direction. So I encourage each and every one of you not to start a fire that you can't contain. Let us make God the center of our passion. Stay encouraged, my brothers and sisters.

Prayer: Dear God, help us to keep our passions headed in the right direction, which is focused on you.

GAME PLAN FOR TODAY: A MARRIAGE THAT WORKS

First Corinthians 13:4–6 says, "Love is patient, love is kind, it does not envy, it does not boast, it is not proud, it is not rude, it is not self-seeking, it is not easily angered, and it keeps no record of wrongs."

There is a quote from a famous movie that says "You complete me". Now this sounds very endearing. But we have to remember that only God can complete us. In other words, we can't put that much responsibility on the person that we love. Because in the long run it ends up being too much for someone to bear. Now I bring this up to say, if you are going to get married, you have to be prepared to go to work, because it takes work to make a marriage successful. For example, some people may say, "My marriage is not working," but perhaps this is because they are not working on their marriage. In fact, if some people approached their job the same way they approached their marriage, they would not even have a job. Sometimes marriage is not pretty like a picture—it needs work. Even when things are going well, it still requires work. So many people go into marriage thinking about what they can get out of it. But when you do this, you miss the point of "giving yourself away .So many people want the "gift" of a relationship without the giving that is required in a relationship. Remember marriage is the best thing, but it's not the easiest thing. So if we understand this and we understand that only God can complete us, then we will be blessed in our marriages and live happily ever after. Stay encouraged, my brothers and sisters.

Prayer: Loving Father, help us to continue to work on our relationships the same way we work on anything that we love in life.

GAME PLAN FOR TODAY: ANXIOUS FOR NOTHING

Philippians 4:7 says, "And the peace of God, which transcends all understanding, will guard your hearts and minds in Christ Jesus."

We all worry about things from time to time, but it will get us nowhere. Worry will cloud your mind and keep you from making the decisions that you need to make right now, in the present. Worry does absolutely no good. It does not solve your problems; in fact, it could actually increase your problems. So the thing we need to start doing is to replace our worries with prayer. You see, a healthy mind is not a confused mind. If we are "in touch" with God, we won't be confused. God is not the author of confusion. If we want to hear from God, we need to keep our minds in a peaceful state, and to do this we have to pay attention to our thoughts. Today, what thoughts are weighing you down? It's time that we all realized that the enemy doesn't want your stuff; the enemy wants your peace. Stay encouraged, my brothers and sisters.

Prayer: Dear God, help us to replace our worries with prayers and thanksgiving.

GAME PLAN FOR TODAY: GETTING WHAT YOU WANT

Proverbs 3:6 says to "submit to God in all your ways, and He will make your path straight."

In my experience, there are two types of people in life—the ones who get what they want and the ones who don't. So I encourage each and every one of you to get what you want. Now the way we accomplish this is submitting our lives to God. I believe everything in your life changes when you make the decision to pursue whatever God has gifted you to do. You see God has a plan that is uniquely yours. However, there are so many talented people that never accomplish the goals that they set. Now this can happen for any number of reasons. One of the reasons I believe is, they do not realize that there will be obstacles along the way. Remember the phrase in a song that goes "Nobody told me that the road would be easy". So we have to remember that our success doesn't come in a straight line. There will be detours along the way. There will be failures along the way. But remember that failures can be the most powerful tool that we use, if we use it to make ourselves better. You see whenever we are on our way to spiritual, emotional, physical, and financial freedom there will be detours. But when we submit to God, he will make our paths straight and our directions clear. So, which person do you want to be, the one who seizes the opportunities no matter what the obstacle is, or the one who allows the failures of life to take you off the road that God has placed you on? Stay encouraged, my brothers and sisters.

Prayer: Heavenly Father, grant me the spiritual discernment to pursue the things that you have gifted me to do.

GAME PLAN FOR TODAY: WHAT'S HOLDING YOU BACK

Second Corinthians 10:5 says we should "take captive every thought to make it obedient to Christ."

You know there is one thing to hold on to a thought in your mind, but it's another thing when a thought holds you captive. Sometimes it can get so bad, that you can't do anything productive. But like this scripture is saying we have to take control of our thoughts. Because there are thoughts that we think about, that are holding us back from being successful. Thoughts like "I'm not good enough" or "I'm not smart enough" or "I'm not spiritual enough." All these thoughts are not from God, they are from the adversary. When these thoughts get in our minds it causes us to see ourselves as failures. This is a lie. I believe that we all need to look at our failures from a spiritual prospective. You see, sometimes we think that the opposite of success is failure, but it's not in the spiritual sense. Because we all fail sometimes. But to me the opposite of success is disobedience to God's calling for your life. So if you are faithful and obedient to what God has called you to do, even your failures will work. So don't let negative thoughts like fear of commitment keep you from getting the job that you desire to have. Because that same fear will keep you from having the relationships that you should have in your life. It can also keep you from the promise and the destiny that God wants you to have. Remember the mind is a terrible thing to waste, so don't let the enemy hold you back with thoughts that are not from God. Stay encouraged, my brothers and sisters.

Prayer: Loving Father, help us to fill out minds with good thoughts.

GAME PLAN FOR TODAY: BE ENCOURAGED

Joshua 1:9 says, "Have I not commanded you? Be strong and courageous. Do not be afraid and do not be discouraged, for the Lord your God will be with you wherever you go."

In my experience, God want give you a purpose without preparing you for it. All your life and throughout all your experiences, God was preparing you for His purpose. Now His promises to you may not come when you want them to, so we all have to learn to be patient. But God is always on time. If you really believe this, then you can embrace anything that comes into your life. Just look at the life of Joshua. I'm sure that he wasn't ready to lead a whole nation of people, but God gave him the encouragement that he needed. You see, God is bigger than any giants that we may face in life. All we have to do is be in fellowship with him. But sometimes no matter how much God encourage us, it's hard for us to keep ourselves encouraged. Even Joshua appeared to have doubts. So it is my belief that the progress that we make in life is up to us. Discouragement is a choice that we make. That's why it's so important for all of us to learn to encourage ourselves. Like the songs says, "sometimes you have to look at yourself in the mirror and tell yourself that you can make it". Also it's okay to pat yourself on the back sometimes. Let us all learn to speak life over our lives and watch things turn around. Always remember, life and death lie in the power of your tongue (Proverbs 18:21). Stay encouraged, my brothers and sisters.

Prayer: Dear God, help me to be encouraged about the plan that you have for my life.

GAME PLAN FOR TODAY: BEING ACCOUNTABLE

Romans 14:12 says everyone who stands before God will have to give an account for their own life.

Sometimes it's easier to tell someone else what to do than it is to take that advice and apply it to your own life. In other words it's easy for me to say don't eat this or you need to work out more or read your bible more. But we all need to be accountable for our own actions. We need to stop saying things like "they made me mad, or they made me do something that I didn't want to. It's time to take responsibility for your life. But applying this idea to our lives requires discipline and self-control. You see, we all need to realize and understand that it's not just hearing the truth that makes you free; it's applying the truth to our lives that makes you free. James 1:22 says," Do not merely listen to the word and deceive yourselves. Do what it says". You know all those people that you thought that you needed to change while you were here on earth? God is not going to ask you one question about them when you get to heaven. So remember that our walk with God is not about everybody else when it comes to our intimate relationship with God and we should treat it as such. Because God has chosen you to let your light shine so that others can see the good things that He has done with you (Matthew 5:16). Stay encouraged, my brothers and sisters.

Prayer: Dear God, help us to be accountable for our own actions.

GAME PLAN FOR TODAY: ACCORDING TO HIS PURPOSE

Romans 8:28 says, "And we know that in all things God works for the good of those who love Him, who have been called according to his purpose."

If we know the character of God, then anything that He asks us to go through has some good purpose for us to get out of it, even though it may seem difficult at the time. For example, Moses obviously didn't want to lead a nation out of bondage, because he realized the magnitude of the situation. But remember—God doesn't call the qualified; God qualifies the called. Joseph realized that what his brothers meant for harm, God meant for good (Genesis 50:20). Sometimes we need to understand that we need more than just information; we also need revelation for our lives. That's why we need to just pray and ask God "what is your purpose for this situation that I am going through. That way we can rest assure that even when things don't look good, He will work a lot of good out of it. Remember—God want always get you out of something, that you got yourself into, perhaps from some bad choices, but He will bring you through something, for His glory. When we partner with God, and stay inside of his good and perfect will, things have a way of working out for our good. Stay encouraged, my brothers and sisters.

Prayer: Heavenly Father, help us to bring you glory according to the purpose that you have for our lives.

GAME PLAN FOR TODAY:
STRONG FINISH

Philippians 3: 12–13 says, "Not that I have obtained all this, or have already arrived at my goal, but I press on to take hold of that for which Christ Jesus took hold of me." It goes on to say, "Forgetting what is behind and straining toward what is ahead."

You know, just because we had a bad start in life doesn't mean that we can't have a strong finish. No matter where you are right now or what you have done or what's been done to you, God has a great plan for your life. All you have to do is allow God with the love of Jesus to come into your life and He will walk you out of your mess and into the abundant life that He wants you to have. But how can we do this? And how do we overcome past regrets that we can't seem to shake? First, we need to make better choices than we did before. Second, we can start surrounding ourselves with a better group of people. Because, show me your friends and I will show you your future. Paul said it like this, "Forgetting what is behind and straining toward what's ahead. Remember whatever is in the past, is supposed to be in the past. I truly believe that we can all come out of whatever circumstance that we are in by making better choices. It's time to take hold of the life that is truly life. This is the life that Jesus died for us to have. But to do this we need to get rid of some things that are keeping us in a place of stagnation. Things like our selfish desires. You see it's our own fleshy desires that keep us from finishing the race that God has for us. We just have to believe that with God all things are possible (Matthew 19:26) and we can turn our circumstances around and a have the strong finish that God desires for us. Stay encouraged, my brothers and sisters.

Prayer: Most merciful Father, help us to realize that we can't do anything about the past, but we can have a strong finish if you will help us make better choices

GAME PLAN FOR TODAY:
THE PURPOSE FOR OBEDIENCE

In Joshua chapter 6, God commands Joshua and the Israelite army to march around the city of Jericho for six days, then on the seventh day give a loud shout. And when they did, the walls came tumbling down. But before the seventh day, not one brick fell.

When we look at this scripture we need to realize that it was the obedience of the Israelite army that allowed God to work this miracle. Because the city of Jericho was what people called a "walled city," which made it impossible to defeat. Many times in our lives we will come up against challenges that make it impossible for us to defeat as well. But when you believe in Gods power you will be sure of the fact that there is nothing impossible for God. Because you will remain faithful no matter what the situation is. You see it is our unbelief that weakens our faith. Just think for a moment how this story would have ended had the Israelite army been disobedient. Unbelief leads to disobedience. Joshua believed that God would do what He said He would do. Which was to make the walls come tumbling down, but once we begin to doubt and not trust in the power of God, we will always end up disobeying what God has planned for our lives. You see, there is nothing that God tells us to do that is for Him; it's always for us. Everything that He tells us to do is so our lives can be better. So anything that He asks us to go through, there will be a "purpose" for us to get something out of it, even though it may seem difficult or unbelievable at the time. Stay encouraged, my brothers and sisters.

Prayer: Loving Father, help us to be obedient to the plan that you have for our lives.

GAME PLAN FOR TODAY: BE PATIENT

James 1:3–4 says, "Knowing that the testing of your faith produces patience. But let patience have its perfect work, that you may be perfect and complete, lacking nothing."

P atience is one of the most important virtues that we can develop as Christians, because it says a lot to people about the "stability" in our lives. We all need to realize and understand that our progress does not always come in a straight line. There will be detours along the way. And sometimes the easiest route in life is not always the quickest route. Many times when things are not easy for us, we tend to complain. Impatience causes us to complain. When we complain, we remain in our same circumstance. You see, it was their impatience that kept the Israelites in the wilderness for forty years. Patience is one of the fruits of the spirit, and it has to do with character and temperament. It has to do with not getting angry when we don't get our way. It also has to do with staying pleasant in an unpleasant situation.

Remember—patience is not just waiting; it's also how we act while we are waiting. Stay encouraged, my brothers and sisters.

Prayer: Heavenly Father, help us to learn to be patient in every situation that we face.

GAME PLAN FOR TODAY: FROM BLAMING TO CLAIMING

Psalm 32:5 says "Then I acknowledged my sin to you and did not cover up my iniquity. I said I will confess my transgressions to the Lord, and you forgave the guilt of my sin."

Sometimes we will never get to the heart of our problems in life until we stop blaming others for our circumstances. So often we will point the finger at someone else for our own bad choices. David understood this principle after a finger was pointed at him that revealed the truth about his situation. It was so revealing that it inspired him to write this beautiful psalm that explains him finally accepting responsibility for his own actions. The reason God forgave David was because he admitted that he was wrong. He finally realized that you will never get clean until you come clean. How many times in our own lives do we place the blame on someone else, when we know it was our own bad decision that caused the outcome. So it's time to go from blaming to claiming responsibility for our own actions. We do this by facing and accepting the truth. Not just any truth, but the truth about ourselves. Also remember that things may happen to us, and there may be reasons why we are the way that we are, but that doesn't give us an excuse to stay that way. Because the moment a reason becomes an excuse, we become "trapped" in it. But once we face the truth about ourselves, we can begin to feel better about ourselves and allow the healing to begin so that we can have the abundant life that Jesus died upon a cross for us to have. Stay encouraged, my brothers and sisters.

Prayer: Most gracious and loving father, help us to take responsibility for the choices that we make in our lives.

GAME PLAN FOR TODAY: NO REGRETS

Philippians 3:13 says, "The one thing I do, forgetting what is behind and straining toward what is ahead."

You know, the great thing about the past is you don't have to feel guilty about it. What we should do is learn from it and move on with our lives. We can't allow a few bad choices that we've made affect the rest of our lives. This is a trap from the enemy. You see, when we finally choose the life that God wants us to have, we should have no regrets about whatever we have done in our lives. When you live with regret, it sucks the life right out of you and keeps you in a state of depression and discouragement. It also keeps you from making the best of your time. Time is too valuable to waste, and the older you get, the faster it goes by. What lies ahead is the new life God wants you to have, with no regrets. He's ready to give you beauty for ashes. He's ready to give joy for your mourning. It's never too late for you to say, Lord, make me over and make me who you want me to be, with no regrets. Stay encouraged, my brothers and sisters.

Prayer: Loving Father, help me to learn from the mistakes that I have made and not live with regrets.

GAME PLAN FOR TODAY: THE ABUNDANT LIFE

John 10:10 says, "The thief comes only to steal and kill and destroy; But Jesus said I came that they may have life and have it abundantly."

We should all learn to live life on purpose and for a purpose. God has given us all free will, and He gave it to us out of His love for us. He wants us to choose His good and perfect will for our lives. And when we do this, we can have the abundant life that He wants us to have. Therefore, every day of our lives, we should be fulfilling the call of God and be the very best version of ourselves that we can be. This means being more loving and kind to people. It means having self-control in difficult situations. It means being at peace with yourself as well as one another. And it means to be faithful to the one that "came" so that we can enjoy a rich and satisfying life. Also, remember that we are not in a relationship with God so that we can get everything we want. We should be in a relationship with God to serve Him and bring Him glory. Stay encouraged, my brothers and sisters.

Prayer: Gracious God, thank you for sending your one and only son so that we can enjoy a rich and satisfying life according to your will.

GAME PLAN FOR TODAY: THE NARROW PATH

Matthew 7:14 says, "Small is the gate and narrow the road that leads to life, and only a few find it."

As we read this scripture, it seems to suggest that most of us would rather do the easy things in life rather than deal with the hard things. This scripture also suggest that, most of us would rather hang with the crowd, no matter what direction that they are going because, surely everybody can't be wrong? So it's easier to walk on the broad path. It's easier to not read the bible on a daily basis. It's easier to not find time to pray. But remember, just like the bible teaches us, it only leads to destruction. I believe that everybody needs some kind of spiritual covering that comes from hearing the word of God every once and awhile. It could be on the radio or on television or you can watch sermons on You Tube, but it has to come from somewhere. I believe without "spiritual covering", this generation will be lost. Everybody has a choice in everything that we do in life. For example, if you really want to exercise, you will find the time and a way to do it. If you really want to get out of debt, then you will stop spending money that you don't need to spend. Also, if you want to grow spiritually, you will find time to read the word of God. You see, nobody can have everything that they want without any sacrifices. There has to be some give and take. So I believe it's time for us to get on the road that is narrow, because our spiritual lives depend on it. Remember—it's the narrow path that leads to life. Stay encouraged, my brothers and sisters.

Prayer: Loving Father, help us to make the choices in life that keep us on the narrow path that leads us to your righteousness.

GAME PLAN FOR TODAY: BETTER

In Jeremiah 29:11 it says, "I know the plans I have for you, plans to prosper you and not harm you, a plan to give you hope and a future.

You know, God has a long-range plan for each and every one of us. No matter how good things are now, they can be better. No matter how bad things are now, they can get better. You see, God has only one thing in mind for your future, and that's "better." He wants us to be better spiritually, better emotionally, and even better financially. I can remember losing my wife of thirty years and I kept thinking, how can things get better? How can this be God's plan for my life? Because she was only fifty one years old. Now I've learned that many people lose loved ones in their lives and when they do we have to make the decision to either "get busy living or get busy dying". The choice is ours. But the thing that helps is when we partner with God and accept Jesus as our Lord and Savior, nothing can stop his plan for our lives. So no matter what you have been through or what you are going through right now, it is all in his good and perfect will for your life. So let us lean not on our own understanding and trust that God has a great plan for our lives. Stay encouraged, my brothers and sisters.

Prayer: Most merciful God, continue to lead us and guide us through the storms of life and give us the faith that we need to endure.

GAME PLAN FOR TODAY: DON'T WAIT FOR TOMORROW

In John 5:8 Jesus says to the man who had been waiting by the pool for thirty-eight years, "Get up! Pick up your mat and walk."

You know, one of man's greatest tragedies is that he wastes what God has given him on earth. Waste of any kind is sad, and certainly, the waste of someone's life is the saddest of all.

As we read this scripture it talks about a man who was so comfortable with his living conditions (which were not good), that he didn't want to do what was necessary to change it. For thirty eight years he was okay with just being a spectator and not participating in God's plan for his life. Do you know any one like this? Because it's sad when someone ends up in a walker, gray haired and all alone with nothing but regrets. That is not the life that Jesus died for us to have. We as Christians need to be determined not to live our lives like that. The only way not to have regrets tomorrow is to do what is right today. Tomorrow can be a dangerous word, especially if God is dealing with us to do something or change something right now. Procrastination can be the enemy for all of us if we are not careful. So it's time to get up and start doing something with the gifts and talents that God has given us. Don't wait for tomorrow; do it today and it will change your whole life around. Stay encouraged, my brothers and sisters.

Prayer: Heavenly Father, help us to do the things today that will keep us from having regrets tomorrow.

GAME PLAN FOR TODAY: DEEP ROOTS

Mark 4:8 says, "Still other seed fell on good soil. It came up, grew and produced a crop, some multiplying thirty, some sixty, some a hundred times."

If you have ever had the opportunity to work in a garden, you know the difference between good soil and bad soil. Whenever I planted something in bad soil, no matter how much fertilizer I used, I could never get that area of ground to produce the same that it does in good soil. That's why whatever it is that you are planting, it needs to have deep roots, so when it's fully mature it will not lack anything except watering and nurturing. Good soil, allows the roots to grow deeper, so that when the winds and the rains come it can endure any kind of bad weather. This is also true as it pertains to our spiritual lives. The way we receive God's word in our hearts will allow us to grow in such a way that we will also be "complete" and able to endure the storms of life. Also, we don't have to worry about the problems of this world that can uproot and choke out what we believe. That's what having deep spiritual roots is all about. But the problem that so many people have is they don't prepare their hearts and mind to receive the word of God and allow themselves to have "deep roots". But I believe there are ways that we can develop a deeper spiritual relationship with God. It all starts with our soil. In this scripture it talks about how some seed fell on "good soil". Now the soil that Jesus is talking about is us. When we receive his word, meditate on his word and truly understand it, then we will be able to grow spiritually. So first, all we need to do is, develop a routine that involves reading the word of God. Second we need a daily routine that involves prayer. And finally we need to read a daily devotional like "A Champion Game Plan for Life". If all of us will do these things I believe that we can develop "deep roots" and grow more spiritually....Stay encouraged my brothers and sisters.

Prayer: Dear God, give us the deep roots that we need to continue doing what you have called us to do.

GAME PLAN FOR TODAY:
THE FAITH BRIDGE

In Mark 9: 22 A concerned father asked Jesus, "If you can do anything, take pity on us and help us". Because his son had severe mental problems. So Jesus questions him and says, "If you can"? Then he goes on to say, "Everything is possible for one who believes.

Y ou know the problems that so many of us have is our unbelief. Any time we have a challenging situation in our life, our faith will be tested, just like we find with this father in this text. Now there is a "faith bridge" that we need to cross over to handle difficult situations. These are situations that we have to go deeper spiritually to get anything resolved. These are problems that only Jesus can handle. Like we found with the woman with the issue of blood who had been suffering for years until Jesus got involved and healed her with the hem of His garment. Now when we cross this bridge of faith we allow Jesus to come into our circumstance. But our unbelief keeps us from crossing over and staying in a place that God did not intend for us to be. This is when we need to grow in our faith. Matthew 17:20, Jesus said if we have faith as small as a mustard seed, then we can move mountains. Now a mustard seed is small but the life inside of the mustard seed is large. Matter of fact there is a fifteen foot tree inside of a tiny mustard seed. So in order for us to grow our faith, first we need to put life into our faith. Then we need to start putting our belief before our sight. So many people are waiting to see their blessings before they participate. Secondly, we need to stop "not believing". This Father said I believe, but help my unbelief. So we need to stop saying "if you can" and start saying "when you can". Finally, just like this father did, we need to ask Jesus to help our unbelief and the only way to accomplish this is to cross over the "faith bridge" that God has constructed for us......Stay encouraged my brothers and sisters

Prayer: Loving Father, help us to have the faith that we need during difficult times

GAME PLAN FOR TODAY: TURN THE LIGHTS ON

Matthew 5:16 says, "In the same way, let your light shine before others, that they may see your good deeds and glorify your father in heaven."

We as Christians are everywhere—factories, schools, hospitals, auto dealerships—but sometimes people don't notice us because we are not letting our lights shine. But it's time to turn the lights on. We do this by being kind to people, being patient with people, and forgiving people when they do something that offends us. There should be something different about the way we treat people or the way we talk to people or the way we behave around people because we have the love of Jesus inside of us. You see, our responsibility to people is to love them and never to give up on them. This is one of God's most important commandments. To love God and to love our neighbors. When we do this, people will see your good deeds and perhaps want to follow your lead and give God some praise. Stay encouraged, my brothers and sisters.

Prayer: Most Loving Father, help us to be mindful of the people around us that we can influence the most.

GAME PLAN FOR TODAY: A RELATIONSHIP THAT MATTERS

Matthew 16:26 says, "What good will it be for someone to gain the whole world, yet forfeit their soul? Or what can anyone give in exchange for their soul?"

Sometimes we can be so logical that our thinking keeps us from having a relationship with God. For example, some people view religion as a crutch for people who can't manage their lives. But the truth is that those people may not be managing their lives so well either. You may have business success, and you may have money in the bank, and you might be well known, but do you have peace in your life? Do you have the peace that surpasses all human and logical understanding? Do you have righteousness? In other words, are you in right standing with God? You see, when we have a relationship with God, it adds meaning to our lives. When we have a relationship with God, it adds purpose to our lives. Having a relationship with God gives us all a moral foundation for our lives. Because without God there is no joy and there is no hope and there is no peace. Stay encouraged, my brothers and sisters.

Prayer: Most gracious God, help us to understand what it means to have peace in our lives.

GAME PLAN FOR TODAY: THE CERTAINTY OF HOPE

Romans 4:21 says, (Abraham) being fully persuaded that God had power to do what he had promised.

I believe that to receive Gods promises for our lives requires us to be patient. Now being patient means to be able to accept or tolerate delays, problems or suffering, without becoming annoyed or anxious. If you remember the story of Abraham, the bible tells us that he had waited long and endured patiently before receiving his first child and yet he was still full of hope. One could also say that Abraham had the certainty of hope which means, he knew beyond all doubt that God would do what he said he would do. Even though, the situation didn't look like there was anything to be hopeful for. So Abraham had two things working for him. He was patient and he was hopeful. I wonder are we as optimistic as Abraham was when it comes to the promises of God. You see we all need to understand that God knows the exact time for us to have what he wants us to have. So when we "partner" with God we need to learn how to be patient. Because the only thing that keeps us from receiving the promises of God is, we give up on the journey. I have learned that our destination is not the most important thing. I found that the journey is the most important thing. But we have to learn how to enjoy the journey and not just endure the journey. So let us all learn to stay full of hope until we reach our destination.......Stay encouraged my brothers and sistersPrayer: Heavenly Father, help us to learn how to be certain beyond all doubt about the promises that you have for our lives.

GAME PLAN FOR TODAY: WINNING THE SPIRITUAL BATTLES

Ephesians 6:12 says, "For we wrestle not against flesh and blood, but against principalities, against powers, against the rulers of the darkness of this world, against spiritual wickedness in high places."

Our thoughts and our words are extremely important. And when we think about something long enough, we will eventually act on it. Where the mind goes, the man (or the woman) will follow. Any thought that we have that doesn't agree with the word of God is not from God. If we want to overcome evil thoughts, we have to learn how to replace them with better ones. And the way that we do this is to learn the word of God so we can defeat the enemy on a spiritual level.

When Jesus was in the wilderness being tempted, He used the word of God to overcome what the devil was trying to tempt Him with. And we need to be able to do the same thing when we are being attacked spiritually. You see, we can only use God's words to fight our battles when we know them.

So we need to meditate on them until they become part of us. Stay encouraged, my brothers and sisters.

Prayer: Awesome God, teach us how to win our spiritual battles by using your words.

GAME PLAN FOR TODAY: CHANGE IS GOOD

James 1:2 says, "Consider it pure joy, my brothers, whenever you face trials of many kinds because you know the testing of your faith develops perseverance."

Once we enter a relationship with God, it causes us to constantly change for the better. Sometimes we may not like the changes in our lives, but it's always for our good. You see, God will do something to you before He can do something through you. So if we are not prepared to be patient, then we don't need to get into a relationship with God, because He is looking for people with a made-up mind who are going to be in it for the long haul. That word "continue" is a very strong word, because it's easy to start something, but much harder to finish. So let us all celebrate the progress that we are making and stop moaning about the rest of the work that has to be done. Stay encouraged, my brothers and sisters.

Prayer: Father God, help us to realize the changes in our lives that make us better.

GAME PLAN FOR TODAY: BE THANKFUL

Philippians 4:6-7 says, "Do not be anxious about anything, but in everything, by prayer and petition, with thanksgiving, present your request to God. And the peace of God that transcends all understanding will guard your hearts and your minds in Christ Jesus."

One of the ways we prepare for increase or promotion in our lives is to be thankful for what we already have. Let us not forget to be grateful for what God is already doing in our lives and for the talents that He has already given us. When we are thankful, we create an atmosphere and a spirit of joy and peace that brings us inner strength. When we are thankful, we guard our hearts and minds against the spirit of complaining about what we don't have. You see, we all have to be careful about complaining, because when we complain, we remain stressed out and in a place where no progress can be made. Remember—life is about momentum, so don't let the enemy keep you from your blessings or from the increase that

God wants you to have by complaining about what you don't have. Stay encouraged, my brothers and sisters.

Prayer: Heavenly Father, help us to be thankful for the gifts and talents that we are already blessed with and give thanks always.

GAME PLAN FOR TODAY: PAYDAY

First Corinthians 15:58 says, "Therefore, my dear brothers and sisters, stand firm. Let nothing move you. Always give yourselves fully to the work of the Lord, because you know that your labor in the Lord is not in vain."

If you have a job, you get excited about "payday." If you don't have a job, then payday is not so exciting. But every Christian has a job, whether we are in full-time ministry or not—we work for God. And every day we need to get up and go into the world and work for God. We do this in the way we talk to people, the way we treat people, the way we behave around people and demonstrate our good attitude. All these things are considered "working" for God. And there will always be a "payday," because God rewards those who diligently seek him. Galatians 6:9 says, "Let us not become weary in doing good, for at the proper time we will reap a harvest if we do not give up." Stay encouraged, my brothers and sisters.

Prayer: Most gracious and loving Father, help us to realize that anything that we do for your glory will be rewarded.

GAME PLAN FOR TODAY:
THE SETUP

James 4:7 says;" Submit yourselves, then to God. Resist the devil, and he will flee from you"

The enemy will always keep us stirred up about something, but we need to resist him from the very beginning. We all see what's going on in our nation today. We see political unrest. We see people in positions of authority killing the very people that they have sworn to protect. We are beginning to hear rumors of war. Everywhere we go, there is tension in the air. It's hard to keep from being offended by the things that are going on right now. But we as believers need to realize that the enemy sets us up to get us upset, and so many of us are playing right into his hands. But it's time to wake up and realize what the devil is trying to do. He is trying to get our attention off what we are called to do, which is to go and make disciples of all the world. Always remember that the enemy doesn't want our "stuff." The enemy wants our peace, and peace is power. Therefore, as long as we live in this world, we will all have trouble and unrest. But Jesus said in John 16:33, "Cheer up, for I have overcome the world." And I leave you with my peace. So let us not get distracted by the troubles of this world because the distraction will set you up to get you upset. Stay encouraged, my brothers and sisters.

Prayer: Most merciful God, help us to not get so upset over the things of this world and to realize that you are still in control.

GAME PLAN FOR TODAY: MAKE TIME

In Matthew 6:33, it says, "But seek ye first the kingdom of God and His righteousness, and all these things will be added unto you."

Today, we live in a society where everybody is so busy, whether at work, with all the demands of our jobs, or at home, with all the demands of our families. Or perhaps you are a student who never has enough time in the day to do the things that you really enjoy doing. Whatever the reasons, there never seems to be enough time, right? But remember— what we put our time, effort, and money into becomes what's important to us. If we say that we don't have time to spend with God, then God is obviously not important in our lives. So let us not deceive ourselves. Anything you really want to do, you will find time to do. I have learned that God is a maximum-capacity God. If you give Him five minutes of your time, He will fill it up. If you give Him thirty minutes of your time, He will fill that up as well. Whatever time you set aside for Him will be worth your while. Remember—God will always meet you where you are, but refuses to leave you there.

So I encourage you to start today, because it will change your life forever. Spending time with God gives our lives meaning and purpose. Stay encouraged, my brothers and sisters.

Prayer: Dear God, give us a willing spirit that will allow us to spend quality time with you.

GAME PLAN FOR TODAY: GOOD FRUIT

Matthew 7:15–16 says, "Beware of false prophets, (people) who come to you in sheep's clothing, but inwardly they are ravenous wolves." You will know them by their fruit.

So many people choose to live a life of compromise. They may say that they are Christian, but their actions are far from it. For example, it's really unfortunate when Christians stay angry all the time, because it hurts our witness. We can't afford to be like the rest of the world and compromise our religious beliefs. This is because the world is watching us and listening to us when we face trials of any kind, just to see how we will react. Now, we all get angry from time to time, but it's what we do and how we behave that is important. Also, we as Christians need to avoid complaining all the time. Once again, complaining affects our witness, because you never know, someone may be watching and listening to you, someone who may be in the process of becoming a new believer. Stay encouraged, my brothers and sisters.

Prayer: Dear God, help us to be aware of the things that we do and say, so that we don't cause others to stumble or fall.

GAME PLAN FOR TODAY: GETTING YOUR PRIORITIES IN ORDER

Matthew 6:21 says, "For where your treasure is, there your heart will be also."

So many of us need to reevaluate our priorities. We need to reevaluate what's important in our lives. Then we can choose with confidence the very best part of life that God has to offer. Things are constantly changing in our lives—in our relationships, in our families, in our jobs. Everything seems to change. And because of these changes, we tend to lose focus of what's really important. Like our relationship with God and the purpose that He has for our lives. You see, we need constantly to be straightening out our priorities so they will stay straight. Therefore, it's time for us to hit the reset button and get our priorities in order. Let us not "cave in" to worldly pressures, thinking that we need a lot of material things to bring us joy. The things that we treasure the most in this world will be meaningless in heaven. That's why so many people have realized that nothing really matters except a relationship with God. Stay encouraged, my brothers and sisters.

Prayer: Loving Father, help us to keep our priorities in order even though things are changing around us.

GAME PLAN FOR TODAY: FORGIVING YOURSELF

Psalm 103:12 says, "As far as the east is from the west, so far has He removed our transgressions from us."

God knows that we are not perfect. He just wants us to keep working toward perfection. He wants us to keep making progress and moving forward. Momentum is everything as it pertains to your spiritual growth. Keep moving forward and don't look back. Don't look back at past disappointments. Don't look back at past mistakes and bad choices that you've made, because you can't do anything about them now. Let's stop looking back at past sins and know in our hearts that God has forgiven us. Isaiah 43:19 says, God is doing a new thing in your life. Can't you perceive it? God is a God of forgiveness and progress. And He wants all of us to be better. Now, I realize that sometimes we may feel unforgiven for our past sins. But that's not the kind of God that we serve.

Remember that Isaiah 43:25 says, "I even I am He who blots out your transgressions for my own sake and remembers your sins no more." When Jesus died on a cross, He paid a debt that none of us could pay, and because of it, our sins were forgiven. Stay encouraged, my brothers and sisters.

Prayer: Most merciful God, help us to realize that our sins are forgiven because of the debt that Jesus paid when He died upon a cross.

GAME PLAN FOR TODAY: ARE WE THERE YET?

Genesis 8:22 says, as long as the earth endures, seedtime and harvest time will never cease.

The reason I like this scripture is that it helps me to understand that "time" is just as important as the "seed." You can't grow anything without the seed. And it takes time for the seed to grow and mature. I remember taking my family to the beach when my daughters were young. It was about a six-hour drive. So every two hours they would ask the question, "Are we there yet?" Often we ask God the same thing as it pertains to our spiritual growth. Or as it pertains to our financial growth. Or even as it pertains to growth in our maturity. No matter what the situation is, we ask God the question, "Are we there yet?" When can I see the fruits of my labor? "Are we there yet?" When can I see a difference in my relationship with my spouse? "Are we there yet?" When will I see a difference in my children's behavior? "Are we there yet?" When will I see a change at my job? "Are we there yet?" In times like these, we have to remember that when we enter a relationship with God, we have to learn to be patient. Just as I would tell my daughters to" just enjoy the ride." Remember in the words of King Solomon, "There is a time for everything". (Ecclesiastes 3:1). That's why we all need to understand this principle of patience. Just enjoy what God is doing in our lives. Because sometimes the more we focus on the outcome, the less we enjoy the journey. Stay encouraged, my brothers and sisters.

Prayer: Dear God, help us to learn to be patient while you are working in our lives.

GAME PLAN FOR TODAY: GOOD INTENSIONS

First Samuel 17:48 says, "As Goliath moved closer to attack, David ran quickly toward the battle to meet him and slain him."

Have you ever had a really good thought to pursue something, but never followed through with it? For whatever reason you talked yourself out of it. Or you let someone else talk you out of it. So many people today have "good intentions" but never take the initiative to do what they are capable of doing. It can be easy to get into the habit of saying, "I'm going to do this or that" but never really following through with it. In the text (1 Sam 17), we find that David took the initiative to step out, in faith, to slay the mighty Goliath, and when he did, it affected a whole nation of people, because no one else would do anything about this giant of a man named Goliath. Also can you imagine how our lives would have been if Jesus had decided not to go to the cross. Remember He had the chance when he was praying to God to "let this cup pass from me, but not my will your will be done". (Matthew 26:39) Procrastination is the enemy of so many people and will keep you in a place of complacency that will not provide the abundant life that Jesus died for us to have. You see, it's not enough to have "good intentions"; you also have to take the initiative and take that step of faith and watch God do the rest. Stay encouraged, my brothers and sisters.

Prayer: Dear God, help us to have more than just good intentions when we are faced with trials of many kinds.

GAME PLAN FOR TODAY: THE CHOICE IS YOURS

Deuteronomy 30:15 says, "See I set before you today life and prosperity." Then it goes on to say in 30:19, "Now choose life, so that you and your children will live."

Your life is headed somewhere with a purpose. And that could be good or bad, the choice is yours. You see, there are two things that we all possess: time and the choices that we make. It doesn't matter who you are, what your social status is, or what your ethnicity is; we all have twenty-four hours in a day. Now, what we do with those twenty-four hours is very important when it comes to our ability to make any progress in life. Whether it be spiritual, physical, emotional, or even financial. We all have the same amount of time in a day to be productive or non- productive. So we have to understand that the choices that we make will determine the outcome of our lives.

I once heard someone say that there will always be the "three C's" of life—first the challenge, then the choice, and then the consequences of the choices that we make. So our goal should be to make the best of our time as well as make good choices. Because it's important that we understand and realize that the choices we make every day will lead us to a path of righteousness or destruction. The choice is yours. Stay encouraged, my brothers and sisters.

Prayer: Heavenly Father, give us the discerning wisdom to make good use of our time so that we can make better choices in our lives.

GAME PLAN FOR TODAY: GOD'S PRESENCE IN YOUR LIFE

Psalm 91:1 says, "He who dwells in the shelter of the Most High will rest in the shadow of the Almighty."

There is nothing more valuable than having the presence of God in your life. Because with God's presence comes peace. No matter what the situation that you are in it is easy to place your trust in him. Many soldiers and police officers will keep this scripture close by, because of the difficult times that they face on a daily basis. But we all need the presence of God in our lives. Because when you have God's presence, there is something different about you. You will react differently in difficult situation. When everything around you is in chaos, you still maintain a since of calmness that everyone will notice. Because you won't let your circumstance or your situation get inside you. That's what it means to stay in God's presence. Now, the way we achieve this kind of temperament is by being obedient to God. You see, there is power connected to obedience. Blessings are released when we are willing to sacrifice our time and our resources to God. Blessings are released when we become broken and get rid of our selfish, independent attitudes. I believe that when we do this, we will stay in God's presence. But remember there is a price we pay for being in his presence. The price is simply being obedient to his word and He will give us the peace we need to endure the difficulties and trials of life.... Stay encouraged, my brothers and sisters.

Prayer: Most gracious and loving Father, help us to stay obedient so we can experience your presence in our lives.

GAME PLAN FOR TODAY:
STRENGTH FROM WEAKNESS

Second Corinthians 10:9 says, "For my strength is made perfect in weakness."

We all have things in our lives that we wish we could do better. Some people wish they could sing better. Some wish they were better athletes or better musicians. When we look at the apostle Paul, believe it or not the bible tells us that He wanted to be a better speaker. As bold as he was as a writer, he felt as though he wasn't as good when it came to speaking (2 Corinthians 10:1). But just think, if Paul had been a better speaker, then he would never have written most of the New Testament. So, are you asking God to give you something that he wants you to work out in another way? Or are you leaning and relying on His strength? You see, I believe that God shows us our weaknesses so that we can see His strength revealed in us. Sometimes what God leaves out is just as important as what He puts in us. Because the things that He leaves out makes us all rely more on Him. Also our perceived weaknesses teaches us to work more with others and forces us to use what we do have. So let us thank God for our weaknesses, because when I am weak, He is strong. (2 Corinthians 12:9) Stay encouraged, my brothers and sisters.

Prayer: Father God, help us to realize and understand that your strength is made perfect in our weakness.

GAME PLAN FOR TODAY: SEIZING THE OPPORTUNITIES

Galatians 6:9 says, "Let us not become weary in doing good, for at the proper time we will reap a harvest if we do not give up."

You know, tomorrow's successes are dependent on today's sacrifices. And your faithfulness in one season has everything to do with how you will experience the next season. Sometimes it can be hard to move forward with your spiritual growth unless you learn what God is trying to teach you right now. You see, there is nothing you can do about all the opportunities that you have missed in your life. But now is the time to seize the opportunities that we do have. Grace gives us the ability to pick up the pieces of where we are now and continue to move forward with full confidence that God is working in our lives. So, if you feel like you're going through a "test" right now, that may be good, because the testing of your faith produces patience and perseverance (James 1:3). But in the meantime, we have to be faithful and seize the opportunities that are right in front of us. Stay encouraged, my brothers and sisters.

Most gracious God, help us not to live with regrets but seize the opportunities that are in front of us today.

GAME PLAN FOR TODAY: REALIZING YOUR FULL POTENTIAL

Luke 5:5 Simon, who is later called Peter, says, "Master, we've worked hard all night and haven't caught anything. But because you say so, I will let down the nets."

When Jesus saw Peter fishing, He saw the potential in Peter to do greater things. He saw that he could be a fisher of men. But there was a process that he and the disciples would have to go through. You see, one of the ways we realize our full potential is through our process—the little things that we do every day that help us prepare for the great things that God wants to do in our lives. Our process reveals our potential, especially when it is tied to a purpose. For example, if you are training to run a marathon, there is a process that you have to go through that will help you realize your full potential. Our spiritual journey requires a process as well. And that process involves reading God's word, daily prayer, and meditation, as well as fellowshipping with other believers. Anything in life worth doing has a process. All we need to do is apply our potential to the right purpose. And that purpose is whatever God has gifted you to do. Stay encouraged, my brothers and sisters.

Prayer: Dear God, help us to realize that in order for us to reach our full potential, we have to embrace the process that helps us achieve the goals that you have for us in our lives.

GAME PLAN FOR TODAY: I WILL NOT BE MOVED

Jeremiah 17:8 says, "They will be like a tree planted by the water that sends out its roots by the stream. It does not fear when heat comes; its leaves are always green. It has no worries in a year of drought and never fails to bear fruit."

What does it mean to be rooted? Looking at our scripture, it means a tree with deep roots will not be blown over in a storm. The wind may blow some leaves off the branches. However, if the tree has deep roots, it has a chance to withstand any storm and not be moved. The same can be said of us and our spiritual growth. Because when we are rooted in the truth of God's word, nothing can blow us over and nothing will get us off the path that God has us on.

You see, the thing that distinguishes believers from non-believers is our inner peace. It's our resolve to handle things, which means we will find solutions to problems when they come up. We will settle disputes when they arise, and we will pursue peace. We need to realize and understand that the devil doesn't want our stuff; he wants our peace. So always remember that peace is power, and the more that you protect your peace, the harder it will be for anything to move you. Not hardships, not tragedies, not calamities. No weapon formed against us shall prosper (Isaiah 54:17). Stay encouraged, my brothers and sisters.

Prayer: Dear God, give us deep roots so that we can endure any problems that come our way.

GAME PLAN FOR TODAY: GREAT FAITH

In Matthew 17:20, Jesus said, "Because you have so little faith. Truly I tell you, if you have faith as small as a mustard seed, nothing will be impossible for you."

If you've ever had to fly on a small plane, you know that a lot can happen when the weather turns bad. But if you fly on a big plane, it can fly above most storms. And the same can be said about our faith. If your faith is attached to a big God, you can rise above any storm in life. You can rise above racism. You can rise above hatred and violence. You can rise above any obstacle that the enemy puts in your way. God is saying to all of us, "Face everything and rise up." You see, the only way to move forward in our lives is to look at our future from God's perspective. Our faith gives us the ability to say, "Whatever is next, I'm ready. So it's time to take fear off the throne of your life and replace it with a God who makes all things possible. Stay encouraged, my brothers and sisters.

Prayer: Awesome God, give us the faith that can move any mountain that the enemy puts in our way.

GAME PLAN FOR TODAY: HOLDING ON TO YOUR FAITH

Job 2:9 says, "His wife said to him, 'Are you still holding on to your integrity?'"

We all have challenging times in our lives, times when it seems as though our faith is being challenged. With all the tragedies going on around the country, it can be hard to maintain your faith in God. I believe that there are certain things that your faith has to survive in order to grow. We first have to survive the reaction phase. This is where our emotions are on full display—emotions of anger, sadness, and frustration. But we have to remember that it's only a reaction, a temporary emotion that will pass. Many people lose their faith in the reaction phase and say things like Job's wife, when she said, "Why don't you curse God and die? But Job replied, 'You talk like a foolish woman, Should we accept only good things from the hand of God and never anything bad?'" We've all had good days and bad days, but if we look around and think things over, our good days usually outweigh our bad days, so there is no need to complain. Don't allow the reaction phase get you off track. Remember Philippians 1:6: "He who began a good work in you will carry it on to completion." Stay encouraged, my brothers and sisters.

Prayer: Most gracious and loving Father, help us to hold on to our faith and integrity during our challenging times.

GAME PLAN FOR TODAY: A LIFE ALIGNMENT

Proverbs 3:6 says, "In all your ways acknowledge Him, and He will make your path straight."

Question: Are you allowing God to pull you into the direction that He wants you to go, or are you allowing the distractions and worries of this world pull you into a direction that you don't want to go in? Hopefully, God is pulling you in His direction. You see, we have to learn to stop any "patterns" in our lives that are causing us to gradually be pulled in the wrong direction. When your car is out of alignment it will pull you a certain way, so you have to get it corrected. The same can be said of our spiritual lives. When we allow difficult times to pull us away from the direction that God wants us to go, we need a life alignment so that God can pull us back into the direction that He wants us to go in. So pay attention to whatever new "life patterns" or habits are causing you to stray away from the path that God wants you on. Stay encouraged, my brothers and sisters.

Prayer: Dear God, lead us in the direction that you would have us go whenever we stray from your will for our lives.

GAME PLAN FOR TODAY:
BUCKLE UP

Matthew 8:25-26 says, The disciples went and woke him, saying," Lord, save us! We are going to drown! He replied, "you of little faith, why are you so afraid?" Then he got up and rebuked the winds and the waves, and it was completely calm.

When we look at the seatbelts in a car, we don't necessarily notice how nice they look or what kind of fabric they are made of. We look at them and value them for the security that they provide. When we put our seatbelts on, we expect them to protect us in the case of an accident. This is how it should be in our spiritual lives. When the disciples got into the boat with Jesus, they should have been sure in knowing that they were safe and secure as long as Jesus was with them. We as Christians should be the same way. When we put our hope and trust in God, we should be secure in knowing that God will take care of us. So when the storms of life are raging, like they were with the disciples, we should have this blessed assurance that God is with us. But remember, He didn't say that He would always save us from the storms; He said that He would be with us in the storm. And knowing that He is always there should provide us the security that we need.

You see, when God sent His one and only son to die upon a cross for the whole world, He became our security in the midst of trouble. All we have to do is accept Him and believe in Him, and he will bring security to our lives—just like that seatbelt when we get into our cars. So it's time to "buckle up" with Jesus and put our faith and trust in him and let Him provide the peace and the security that we need for our lives. Stay encouraged, my brothers and sisters.

Prayer: Heavenly Father, help us to put our trust and faith in you when difficult times come in our lives

GAME PLAN FOR TODAY:
A HEART THAT PLEASES GOD

Genesis 4:3–5 says, "In the course of time Cain brought some of the fruits of the soil as an offering to the Lord. And Abel brought an offering, fat portions from some of the firstborn of his flock. The Lord looked with favor on Abel and his offering. But on Cain and his offering, he did not look with favor."

When I played professional football, we were judged by our talents, our strength, our size, and our speed. But God doesn't look at us that way. God looks at our hearts, and He looks at our desire to please Him. As we see here in this scripture, Abel had a greater desire to please God than Cain did. So my question is, do we only desire God to answer prayers for our lives, or do we desire to please Him? So often we want God to answer our prayers, but we don't honor our commitments that we make to God. For example, we may say that we are going to study the word more or pray more or give more, but we never follow through with these promises. So I pray that God gives each and every one of us a more dedicated heart so that we can be more obedient and committed to what He wants us to do. Stay encouraged, my brothers and sisters.

Prayer: Merciful God, give us a clean heart so that we can better serve you.

GAME PLAN FOR TODAY: GETTING THE WEEDS OUT

Matthew 13:27–28 says, "Sir, didn't you sow good seed in your field? Where then did the weeds come from? 'An enemy did this,' he replied."

The other day I was pulling up weeds that had grown in my yard and my plant bed. The reason that they had grown up was that I neglected them and allowed them to grow. You see, I didn't do what I needed to do on a daily basis or weekly basis to keep them out. When you are dealing with weeds, you have to stay on top of things or they will get out of control. The same can be said about our spiritual growth. When we allow the enemy to plant weeds in our lives, they will "choke out our growth." When we allow worrying, bitterness, complaining, and unwholesome talk to be planted in our lives, they act like weeds that need to be pulled up and eliminated from our lives. If we don't, we won't have the beauty that God wants us to have. Since I've pulled the weeds out of my plant bed, everything is beautiful. Everything is the way that God wants it. You see, by getting the weeds out of your life, you can bring God the glory that He is worthy of. Stay encouraged, my brothers and sisters.

Prayer: Dear God, help us to be aware of the weeds that are in our lives so that we can eliminate them.

GAME PLAN FOR TODAY: LOOKING MORE LIKE GOD

The violence that took place in Las Vegas in 2017 made me think about this question. What does God look like to you? In 1 John 1:5, it says "God is light; in him, there is no darkness at all." So if we are believers in God and followers of Christ, we should know what He looks like. Does He look like love (because God is love) or does He carry a gun? Does He look like peace, (because God is peace) or does He advocate violence? You see whenever we see peace, God is there. Whether it be in your marriage or your relationships with your family and friends, God looks like peace. Philippians 4:7 says the peace that surpasses all understanding will guard your hearts and minds in Christ Jesus.

You see, there are a lot of people with messed up minds out there, just waiting to be used by the devil. They don't know what God looks like. They don't know that they are walking in darkness. But I believe that when we walk in love, joy, peace, self-control, and kindness, we represent what God looks like. Remember we are the salt of the earth, and we are the light of the world. We may never understand why people commit such senseless acts of violence, but we all need to start looking more like God and representing Jesus. Stay encouraged, my brothers and sisters.

Prayer: Father God, help us to look more and more like you each day.

GAME PLAN FOR TODAY: COST AND REWARDS

In Luke 18:18, it says, "A certain ruler asked him, Good teacher, what must I do to inherit eternal life?" Jesus answers in verse 22, "Sell everything that you have and give to the poor, and you will have treasures in heaven."

You know, one of the things that we have to realize is that, in this life, there is always going to be a cost for everything that we do, but there are also rewards. For example, if we want to have a healthy relationship with someone, then we need to spend quality time with that person. So your reward will be a satisfying relationship. If you want to get in shape or lose weight, you have to give up certain foods and perhaps work out more, but your reward will be a healthy body. The same can be said in our spiritual lives: there is a cost for following Jesus, but He also provides us with a reward. And that reward is eternal life. Now, being a disciple of Jesus Christ is more than just being forgiven or just coming to church. Being a disciple is the process of moving toward spiritual adulthood. It's conducting yourself in such a way that others can see the good works that God is doing in your life. But it all comes with a price. So we have to watch what we say and watch what we do and watch how we live. You see we may have to pay a price, but God offers a reward. And that reward comes from growing in the knowledge of God. So what must we do to be a follower of Jesus Christ? We need to continue to grow spiritually and believe in the one that God sent. Stay encouraged, my brothers and sisters.

Prayer: Loving Father, help us to understand that the rewards outweigh the cost for following you.

GAME PLAN FOR TODAY: PROVIDING COMFORT FOR OTHERS

2 Corinthians 1:3-4 says, Praise be to the God and Father of our Lord Jesus Christ, the Father of compassion and the God of all comfort, who comforts us in all our troubles, so that we can comfort those in any trouble with the comfort we ourselves receive from God.

You know once again there was another school shooting. Once again no one knows why the shooter decided to kill innocent people. Once again there will be flowers and memorials set in place where peoples loved ones have died. And once again the families will try to seek closure as to why this all happened. In 2 Corinthians 1, Paul wants to tell us the truth. And the fact of the matter is life can be painful. When Jesus died upon the cross, it was painful. We all see that sin has made its ugly mark on society, and its repercussions are felt in a major way. But guess what? We are not alone. There were many people in the bible that endured hardships. For example, Job was a righteous man and yet he still had to endure pain and suffering. The apostle Paul was no stranger to pain either and yet through it all He says I still want to give God praise. You see if we ever want to provide comfort for others, there are some things we need to understand. First, we need to realize that God is sovereign. So no matter what happens in our lives God is still in control, even though there will be mistakes and failures from other people. God is working them out in our lives for our good. Secondly, we need to understand that God will change the condition of your circumstance. For example, God did not simply just deliver the Hebrew boys from the fiery furnace, He joined them in the furnace. So even though the fire was still hot, the fire was not normal, because Jesus, joined them in it. So if God has not taken you out of something, let him join you in it, so that the condition of your situation will change for the better. Stay encouraged my brothers and sisters

Prayer: God of all comfort, help us to provide others with the comfort that you have given us

Printed in the United States
By Bookmasters